Weight W Smart Points Cookbook

Mouthwatering Slow Cooker Recipes for Fast Weight Loss & Healthy Living

BY

KIM HILTON

Table of Contents

Books by The Same Author

- <u>Boost Your Energy Levels:</u> 60 Natural Ways to Get Rid of Fatigue, Dizziness, Weakness, And Lack of Motivation

- <u>How to Get Rid Of Stretch Marks Naturally</u>

- <u>How to Break Sugar Cravings with Nutritional Supplements:</u> Healthy and Natural Alternatives

- <u>The Anti-Anxiety Cookbook:</u> Nutritional Plan to Cure Depression and Anxiety (Stress Relief and Mental Health Cookpot)

- <u>Eating Disorder Recovery Workbook:</u> How to Recover from Eating Disorder

On Your Own (Anorexia, Bulimia Nervosa, And Binge Eating)

Introduction

The recipes provided in this book are based on portion and calorie control. it is a system that will give you a chance to actually eat the regular foods you like without consuming too much fat. Foods provided are aimed to help you lose weight by consuming more fiber and good protein instead of bad fat. Your feeding will never remain the same, and you will be exposed to delicious dishes while you are losing weight. This is the best strategy of dieting in the 21st century, and you should also take part.

With Smart Points for individual recipes, the foods are rated as healthy and the aim is not to make you underweight but to keep you at a healthy weight range, where you will maintain both your health and your energy. You will have the ability to eat and to do the same activity while actively losing weight.

Lemon and Herb Shrimp

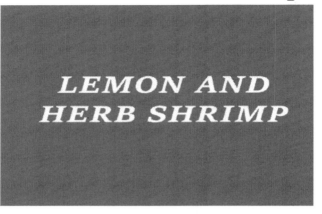

These recipe contains 16 grams of protein, 3 grams of total fat, and 103 calories in total.

Cooking materials:

Chopped, fresh parsley – 2 tablespoon

Freshly ground, black pepper – ¼ teaspoon

Table salt – ½ teaspoon

Herb seasoning – 1 teaspoon

Lemon juice, fresh – 2 tablespoon

Deveined and peeled shrimp – 1lb large shrimp

Olive oil – 2 teaspoon

Procedures:

Use mild heat to heat oil

After 1 minute, add sauce and shrimp

Add the following:

Pepper

Salt

Lemon herb seasoning

Lemon juice

And stir slowly for 30 seconds

Allow it to cook until the shrimp turn to bright pink color. This will usually occur in 3 minutes.

Stir in parsley after removing from heat.

Roasted Pork Tenderloin with Herbs

This recipe consists of 24 grams of protein, 1g of carbohydrate and total of 5g fat. It contains around 151 calories, by which 46 comes from the fat.

Materials for cooking:

Pork tenderloin, lean – 2lb

Olive oil – 2 teaspoon

Freshly grounded, black pepper – 1 tablespoon

Table salt – 1 tablespoon

Onion powder – 1 teaspoon

Garlic powder – 1 teaspoon

Oregano, dried – 2 teaspoon

Thyme, dried – 2 teaspoon

Cooking spray - single

Direction for cooking:

400F oven preheat

Use cooking spray to coat the roasting pan. The roasting pan has to be preferably shallow.

Combine the following in a small bowl:

Pepper

Salt

Onion powder

Garlic powder

Oregano

Thyme

Spread oil on the pork and rub to make sure it is adsorbed.

Sprinkle the combined mixture as well, on the pork.

Transfer the meat to the roasting pan.

Roast for about 30 minutes. (if you are using the instant read thermometer, you will notice that the pork will read around 160F)

Remove and allow it to cool off for about 10 minutes.

Slice crosswise in order to create thin slices.

Baked Chops with Garlic

This recipe consists of 17 grams of protein, 2g of sugars and 1g of dietary fiber. total fat rests about 1g, which is about 4% of the whole meal. Sodium is 10 percent and cholesterol 15 percent.

Materials for cooking:

Single cooking spray

Garlic powder – 1 dash

Paprika – ¼ teaspoon

Italian seasoning, dried – ¼ teaspoon

Bread crumbs, dried – 1/3 cups

Lightly beating egg white – 1 large

Garlic powder – 1/8 teaspoon

Ginger, ground – ¼ teaspoon

Soy sauce, low sodium - 1 tablespoon

Pineapple juice – 2 tablespoon

"Center-cut lean pork loin chop" – 6 oz.

Directions for cooking:

350-degree C oven preheat

Remove fat from chops by trimming

Combine the following in a bowl:

Egg whites

Garlic powder

Ginger

Soy sauce

Juice

And stir very well.

Also combine the following in a shallow dish:

A dash of garlic powder

Paprika

Italian seasoning

Breadcrumbs

And stir well.

Dip the chops in the juice mixture and remove to be dredged in the breadcrumbs.

Dredge chops in breadcrumbs mixture after dipping in the juice mixture.

Coat the broiler pan with a cooking spray, then place chops.

The chops should be baked at 350 degrees.

"Bake for 50 minutes, but turn at 25 minutes."

Garlic Lemon Scallops

GARLIC LEMON SCALLOPS

This consist of 18 grams of protein, and 1g of saturated fat. Total fat content ranges around 4 grams, which is 6 percent of the whole meal. Sodium is 29 percent, while therein contains 11 percent of cholesterol.

Materials for cooking:

chopped parsley – 2 tablespoon

lemon juice – single

finely chopped scallion – single

minced garlic cloves – 4 to 6

salt – ¼ teaspoon

all purpose flour – two tablespoon

paper towel-dried, sea scallop – 1 ¼ lb.

olive oil – 1 tablespoon

Instructions for cooking:

"heat oil in a large nonstick skillet.

Toss scallops with flour and salt in a medium bowl.

Place the scallops in skillet and add the following:

Sage

Scallions

And garlic

Turn the scallops into opaque by sautéing. Sauté for about 5 minutes.

Add parsley and lemon juice while stirring, and remove from heat.

Serve immediately for total nourishment."

Parmesan Chicken Cutlets

This weight watcher recipe consists of only 5 grams of total fat, amounting into only 7 percent of total food content. It contains 27 grams of proteins, 12 percent of sodium and 26 percent of cholesterol.

Materials for cooking:

One pound of boneless chicken breast – 4

Freshly ground, black pepper – ¼ tablespoon

Garlic powder – ½ teaspoon

Dried parsley – one teaspoon

Paprika – 1/8 teaspoon

Seasoned Italian bread crumbs, dried – 2 tablespoon

Grated parmesan cheese – ¼ cup

Directions for cooking:

400-degree oven preheat

"Combine and shake all seasonings in a resalable plastic bag."

Remove the mixture and put in a plate.

"Coat the chicken breast with the mixture by dipping and turning into the cheese mixture."

"Place a baking sheet and place the chicken breast."

Bake the chicken for 25 minutes.

Serve either hot or warm.

Cheese Soufflé

Materials for cooking:

2 room temperature stored egg white

"Separated with whites, eggs" (also at room temperature)

Cayenne pepper – 1/8 teaspoon

Divided salt – ½ teaspoon

Shredded cheddar cheese (reduced fat) – 1 ½ cup

Divided low fat milk - 1 cup (one percent low fat)

All purpose flour – 3 tablespoon

Directions for cooking:

Mix together the following in a small bowl or cup:

Milk – 3 tablespoons

And flour

Mix the two together until the paste become smooth.

Place a saucepan on a low heat and pour the remaining milk.

Add the flour mixture to the saucepan and stir.

Stir continuously for about 6 mins in order to get a thick mixture, then remove from the heat.

Add the following:

Cayenne pepper

¼ teaspoon

Cheddar cheese

Remove everything and transfer to a bowl for good balance.

Let it cool.

Preheat oven at 175 degrees.

Combine the cooled cheese with egg yolks, whisk very well.

"Put the 4 egg whites on a large metal bowl and whip in order to form foam."

"Add the ¼ teaspoon of salt remaining and beat in order to make it stiff."

"Then, stir the ¼ of the egg whites into the cheese mixture."

Combine the remaining egg whites with the mixture. Make use of spatula in order to get a perfect fold.

Place a soufflé dish (3 quart) and put the mixture.

Bake the mixture for 30 minutes. In 30 minutes you will notice thee soufflé getting puffed, this means it is cooked.

Serve immediately for better nourishment.

Egg Drop Soup with Chicken

This weight watcher also contains only 6 percent of fat, 27 percent of proteins and 20 percent of cholesterol considering you are using direct measurement as provided.

Materials for cooking:

Lightly beaten egg – single

Thinly sliced green onion – ¼ cup

Green peas, frozen – ½ cup

Chopped, skinless chicken breast (boneless and cooked) - ½ cup

Soy sauce – ½ teaspoon

Chicken broth, low sodium – 4 cup

Directions for cooking:

Boil the soy sauce and chicken stock in a saucepan.

Add the following:

Green onion

Pease

And chicken.

Boil again.

Do away with from heat.

Add the egg slowly. Preferably drizzle steadily and allow it to sit for a minute.

Stir smoothly and serve.

Spicy Baked Shrimp

The fat content for this weight watcher is 3 percent, 31 percent protein and 33 percent of sodium.

Material for cooking:

Cooking spray (olive oil-flavored) – single

Deveined and peeled, shrimp – 1lb large

Soy sauce, low sodium – 2 teaspoon

Olive oil – 1 teaspoon

Creole seasoning – 2 teaspoon

Parsley, dried – 2 teaspoon

Honey – 1 tablespoon

Lemon juice – 2 tablespoon

Directions for cooking:

Oven: preheat at 230 degrees C

Use a cooking spray to coat a baking dish (preferably 11x7 inch).

Add the following to the baking dish:

Soy sauce

Olive oil

Creole seasoning

Dried parsley

Honey

Lemon juice

Stir to combine in the dish.

For coating, add shrimp.

Allow to bake for 7 to 10 minutes.

The shrimp will turn pink.

It is important that you stir occasionally in order to achieve a stable mixture.

Serve hot or warm.

Dijon Fish Fillets

DIJON FISH
FILLETS

The weight watchers consist of 2 percent of fat, 41 percent of protein and 12 percent of sodium.

Materials for cooking:

Cooking spray, butter-flavored – single

Bread crumbs, Italian (seasoned) – 2 tablespoon

Worcestershire sauce, reduced sodium –

1 teaspoon

Lemon juice 1 ½ teaspoon

Dijon mustard – 1 tablespoon

Sole fillet – single (1 ounce) - flounder

or orange roughy

Directions for cooking:

Oven: preheat to 230 degrees C

Coat baking dish with cooking spray

(baking dish: 11x7 inch)

Fillets re to be arranged in the coated

baking dish.

Combine the following in a bowl:

Worcestershire sauce

Lemon juice

Mustard

"Stir well and evenly spread over the fillet."

Evenly sprinkle your breadcrumbs as well.

"Bake for 11 minutes until fish flakes. You can discover this when pierced with fork. Also, the baking should be made with the baking dish uncovered."

Can be served immediately, after the fillets are cut into two.

Baked Chicken with Lemon and Herbs

BAKED CHICKEN WITH LEMON AND HERBS

This weight watcher consists of 6 percent fat, 49 percent protein and 19 percent sodium.

Materials for cooking:

Medium lemon – single

Chicken broth – ¼ cup

Chopped, fresh parsley – 2 teaspoon

Chopped, rosemary fresh – 2 teaspoon

Lemon juice, fresh – 2 teaspoon

Olive oil – 1 teaspoon

Freshly ground, black pepper – ¼ teaspoon

Sea salt – ½ teaspoon

Chicken breast – 1 lb. boneless (preferably skinless, and it should be divided into four halves.)

Directions for cooking:

Oven: preheat to 200 degrees C

Use black pepper and sea salt to season chicken.

Use olive oil to drizzle a roasting pan.

Sprinkle the roasting pan with the following:

Parsley

Rosemary

And lemon juice.

"Coat the pan bottom with broth. Just around the chicken."

The chicken and mixture should be baked for 33 minutes. If your heat isn't certain, bake until the chicken is cooked. You can know that by testing the chicken with fork.

Use the fresh lemon for garnish.

Slow Cooker Chili

This weight watcher contains fat as low as 3g, which is about 4 percent of the whole content. It consists of 5 percent of carbohydrate, 20 percent of dietary fiber and 26 percent of protein.

Materials for cooking:

Black pepper – single

Tomato paste – 2 tablespoon

Finely chopped, seeded jalapeno pepper (fresh) – ¼ cup

Chopped, sweet onion – single

Rinsed and drained, kidney beans (red) – 1 can (15 oz.)

Crushed tomatoes – 1 can (28 oz.)

Cumin – 2 teaspoon

Chili powder – 2 tablespoon

Diced and seeded, green bell pepper – 1 large

Diced and seeded, red bell pepper – 1 large

Minced, fresh garlic – 1 teaspoon

Ground beef or turkey – 1 lb. extra-lean

Directions for cooking:

Use a nonstick skillet to cook the turkey or beef.

Cook until the turkey or beef turn brown.

Drain the fat.

Return to the pan.

Cook for about 5 minutes as you add the bell peppers.

Add cumin and chili powder as you stir.

Place the following in a slow cooker:

Meat

Tomato paste

Jalapeno or chilies

Onion

Kidney beans

Tomatoes

And stir in order to combine.

Cook for 5 hours.

Cover while cooking in order to maintain a good and combined flavors.

Use black pepper as a taste seasoning.

Turkey Sausage and Bell Peppers

It contains 12 percent of protein, 16 percent of sugars, 13 percent of sodium and only 4 percent of fat.

Materials for cooking:

Oregano, dried – ¼ teaspoon

Red pepper flakes, crushed – ¼ teaspoon

Minced garlic – 2 tablespoon

Chicken broth – ¼ cup

Sliced onion – single

Sliced bell pepper, yellow – single

Sliced bell pepper, green – single

Sliced bell pepper, red – single

Slices of Italian turkey sausage – ¼ lb.

Directions of cooking:

Heat skillet: spray cooking spray over the skillet before heating. Pam cooking spray is preferable in this case.

Add sausage to the skillet.

Stir for 5 minutes until the skillet is no longer pink.

Add the following:

Oregano

Pepper flakes

Garlic

Broth

Onion

Bell peppers

Sauté the combined for 6 minutes.

Allow the liquid portion to evaporate, then reduce heat.

Cover for 5 minutes and simmer.

It can be served immediately.

Shrimp with Cilantro and Lime

SHRIMP WITH CILANTRO AND LIME

The percentage of protein is 54, and has a total fat of just 6 g, making about 8 percent.

Materials for cooking:

Pepper – ¼ teaspoon

Salt – ½ teaspoon

Zest lime – 1 teaspoon

Chopped cilantro, fresh – ¼ cup

Olive oil – single tablespoon

Minced, garlic cloves – two cloves

Ginger, ground - ¼ teaspoon

Cumin, ground – ½ teaspoon

Lime juice, fresh – 2 tablespoon

Peeled, large shrimp (deveined) – 1 ¾ lb.

Instructions for cooking:

Combine the following in a large bowl:

Garlic

Ginger

Cumin

Lime juice

Shrimp

Toss them very well.

Over a mild heat, heat the oil (nonstick skillet are preferably used).

Put the combined (shrimp) mixture n the skillet

Sauté for 5 minutes. Sometimes the shrimp might be done before 5 minutes, you can remove the heat.

Add the following when you remove from heat:

Pepper

Salt

Lime zest

Cilantro

"Per serving: 3 SmartPoints; 4 PointsPlus; 4 POINTS (old)"

Tuna Salad

It consists of 20 grams of proteins, which is about 40 percent, 7 percent of total fat, and 1 percent of dietary fiber. also, it has about 28 percent of sodium.

Materials for cooking:

Freshly ground black pepper – ¼ teaspoon

Salt – 1/2

Calorie mayonnaise, reduced – 2 tablespoon

Chopped parsley, fresh – 2 tablespoon

Finley diced celery – ½ cup

"Solid white tuna, canned chunk (liquid drained)" – 12 oz.

Instructions for cooking:

Combine the following in a bowl:

Parsley

Celery

Tuna.

Also add the following (stir):

Pepper

Salt

Mustard

Mayonnaise

You can also add the following in order to increase flavor:

Onions

Relish or chopped pickles

Diced olives

"Per serving: 3 SmartPoints; 3 PointsPlus; 3 POINTS (old)"

Orange Crumbed Baked Chicken

It contains 37 percent proteins, 23 percent cholesterol and 19 percent total fat. It also contains 2 g of fiber, which amounts to 9 percent.

Cooking materials:

Chicken thigh (boneless chicken) – 12 oz.

Freshly ground, black pepper – ¼ teaspoon

Finely chopped shallot – single

Grated, orange zest – 1 tablespoon

Crumbled, whole-wheat crackers – ¾ cup

Salt - ¼ teaspoon

Dijon mustard – 2 tablespoons

Orange juice – two tablespoons

Cooking instructions:

Oven preheat: 350 degrees C

Use a nonstick cooking spray and a nonstick baking sheet.

Spray the nonstick cooking oil evenly on the baking sheet.

Combine the following in a small bowl:

Salt

Mustard

Orange juice

Also, combine the following on a sheet – preferably. Wax paper

Pepper

Shallot

Orange zest

Cracker crumbs

Sprinkle the mustard mixture on the chicken. Make sure that the mixture touches both sides.

Use the crumbs to coat the entire chicken.

Bring the baking sheet to play, and place the chicken on it.

Bake the chicken for 16 minutes to achieve consistency.

5 SmartPoints

Raspberry Balsamic Chicken

Materials for cooking:

Vinegar, balsamic – 1 ½ tablespoon

Raspberry preserves, low sugar – ½ cup

Corn starch – 1 ½ teaspoon

Chicken broth – 2/3 cup (low fat)

All purpose flour – ¼ cup

Pepper, black – single

Salt – single

Chicken breast, boneless – three

Instructions for cooking:

Slice chicken into pieces. The slice should be smaller than normal.

Season with the following:

Black pepper

Salt

Dip in all purpose flour, remove and shake to get rid of excess.

Bake chicken for about 16 minutes.

Heat should be moderate, and the cooking should be done in a non-stick skillet.

Turn the chicken 8 minutes into the cooking time.

Remove from the cooking medium.

Mix the following in the skillet:

Raspberry preserves

Corn starch

Chicken broth

Then place over moderate heat.

Add the balsamic vinegar

Put the chicken back and cook for 12 minutes.

Also, turn the chicken 6 minutes into the cooking time.

Serve immediately

"5 smart points per serving."

Crock Pot Chicken Chili

This recipe contains 28 percent of protein at 14g, 2 percent of fat at 2g and 22 percent of dietary fibre at 6g, with the total carbohydrate content of 24g.

Materials for cooking:

Salsa – ½ cup

Chopped onion – single clove

Chopped bell pepper, green – single

Drained kidney beans – 15 oz.

Undrained corn – 15 oz.

Tomatoes, canned – 1 qtr.

Mixed chilli seasoning – 1 3/8 oz.

Chicken breast, skinless – 12 oz. (it should be diced)

Instructions for cooking:

Make use of cooking spray all over a cooking skillet.

"Sear the chicken"

Add the following in a crock pot:

Salsa

Onion

Green bell pepper

Kidney beans

Corn

Tomatoes

Chili seasoning mix

Chicken

Cook in a covered pot for about 7 hours

Serve immediately

"5 smart points per serving."

Oven Fried Fish

It contains 48 percent of protein, at 24g, 10 percent of total fat, and 2 percent of dietary fiber.

Materials for cooking:

Melted butter – 3 tablespoon

Milk, skim – 1/3 cup

Paprika – ½ teaspoon

Pepper, black – 1/8 teaspoon

Salt – ½ teaspoon

Dill, dried – ½ teaspoon

Bread crumbs – ¼ cup

Cornmeal, yellow or white - ¼ cup

Fish, white (tilapia fillets or fresh haddock) – 1 ½ lb fresh

Cooking instructions:

Oven preheat: 450 degrees

"Combine seasoned ingredients in a dish (dish should be preferably shallow)"

Pour the right amount of milk in an open dish

Dredge the fish in the milk.

Remove the fish and sire in the crumb

"After coating the fish with the cooking spray, place in a pan."

Use melted butter to drizzle.

Cook the fish for just 10 minutes.

You can taste the fish within that period with a fork to check if it is baked.

"5 smartpoints per serving."

Quick Chicken Noodle Soup

Materials for cooking:

Pepper, black – single

Salt – single

Parsley, dried – ¼ teaspoon

Thyme, dried – ¼ teaspoon

Thinly sliced onion – 8 cloves, green

Chopped celery – ½ cup

Chopped carrot – ½ cup

Spaghetti, thin – 1 cup

Chicken broth, fat free – 5 cups

Chicken breast – 8 oz. (to be cut into pieces)

Instructions for cooking:

Use the following to season chicken:

Black pepper

Salt

Sprinkle a cooking spray on a skillet.

Place the skillet on a moderate to high heat.

Put the chicken immediately and allow it to cook for 4 minutes.

Stir through the time of cooking to make sure that every part is getting the same amount of heat.

Add the following in a soup pot:

Chicken

Parsley

Thyme

Green onion

Celery

Carrots

Spaghetti

Chicken broth

When the mixture starts boiling, check to make sure the spaghetti is soft.

Add black pepper and salt to taste.

"5 smartpoints per serving."

Books by The Same Author

- <u>Boost Your Energy Levels:</u> 60 Natural Ways to Get Rid of Fatigue, Dizziness, Weakness, And Lack of Motivation

- <u>How to Get Rid Of Stretch Marks Naturally</u>

- <u>How to Break Sugar Cravings with Nutritional Supplements:</u> Healthy and Natural Alternatives

- <u>The Anti-Anxiety Cookbook:</u> Nutritional Plan to Cure Depression and Anxiety (Stress Relief and Mental Health Cookpot)

- <u>Eating Disorder Recovery Workbook:</u> How to Recover from Eating Disorder On Your Own (Anorexia, Bulimia Nervosa, And Binge Eating)

Printed in Great Britain
by Amazon